The Penguin

A Funny Bird

Text by Béatrice Fontanel
Photos by André Fatras and Yves Cherel

Charlesbridge

Copyright © Editions Milan 1989.
300 rue Léon Joulin 31101 Toulouse, France.
Original edition first published by Editions Milan under the title of *le manchot, drôle d'oiseau*.

Copyright © 1992 by Charlesbridge Publishing.
Library of Congress Catalog Card Number 92-70578
ISBN: 0-88106-426-2
Published by Charlesbridge Publishing, 85 Main Street, Watertown, MA 02172 • (617) 926-0329
All rights reserved, including the right of reproduction in whole or in part in any form.
Printed in Korea.
10 9 8 7 6 5 4 3 2 1

Each little white spot is a penguin. They gather together to form huge colonies when it is nesting time.

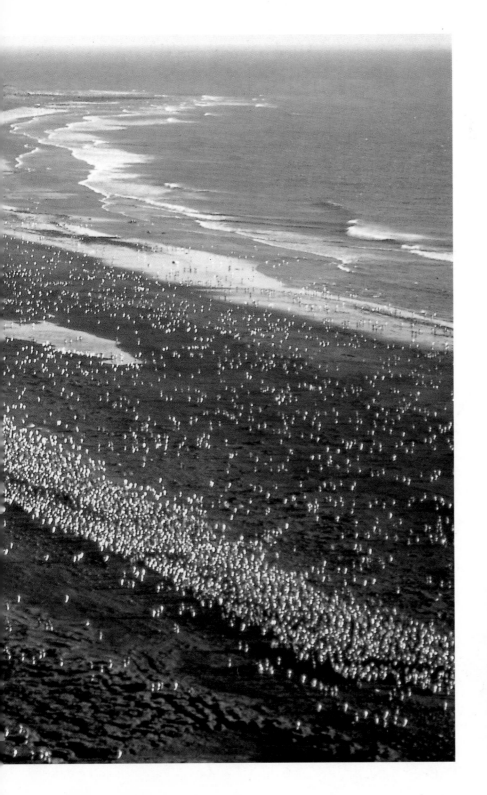

The penguin, a funny bird

At the "bottom" of the world, lies a string of small rocky islands in the Antarctic ocean. Millions of king penguins live there. They cannot fly. These birds stand in the wind and rain chattering so loudly that their noise can be heard from far away.

The orange markings are very special. They help the penguins see that they are all members of the king penguin family.

5

Love Songs

In the southern
hemisphere where the
penguins live, the seasons
are the opposite of ours.
When summer begins in
November, the penguins
leave the ocean where
they have been eating
their fill. All chubby, they
ride the waves and
waddle across the beach
to look for a mate. When
penguins find their mates,
they stand face to face
with their beaks stretched
up to the sky, and their
wings back. Then they
bow to each other and
sing their songs.

Each penguin has its own song. In this
way the male and female are able to
find each other again, even though
there are many thousands of pairs.

It's not easy for penguins to scratch themselves behind the head, but by bending and twisting, they can.

The largest penguin colony in the world has 300,000 couples. The birds travel to this place by following "roads" that have been worn down by penguins walking the same ways over many years.

Even though king penguins live in huge groups, they do not crowd each other. Each one keeps a small area around it, just big enough to stretch out its beak and flap its wings.

In the warm penguin colony

Even in the warm season, huge storms can blow in very quickly. The penguins are well prepared to deal with storms. Their smooth bodies have a thick layer of fat under the skin, and feathers that are layered like the shingles on a roof.

Instead of building nests, the king penguins turn their backs to the wind, and hold their eggs under them. They are very careful to keep the egg from rolling away.

No nest...
and only one egg

The female lays her egg in mid-November. It is as big as a grapefruit and pear-shaped. She places it on its side on her webbed feet! She covers it with a big fold of skin to keep it warm. This must be the strangest cradle in the world.

A few hours after laying the egg, the female penguin must go back to the ocean to eat for two or three weeks. While she is away, it is the male who takes care of the egg. He grows thinner each day. When the female returns, she takes back the precious egg and the male leaves to go eat.

An abandoned penguin egg is a great find for an egg-eating bird like this skua.

When a penguin returns to take care of the egg, it bows and clicks its beak to say "I'm back. It's me. You can have your turn to fish now."

Penguins sometimes lose their eggs after a storm or a flood.

This giant petrel will not attack a big penguin, but it will try to make a meal of a penguin egg or a baby chick.

Hurry! You must keep eating to fatten up as much as possible before the bad weather comes.

One week after birth, the baby shyly goes outside. It has no feathers and is completely helpless.

When a male or female penguin comes back from fishing, it sings its special song. Older babies recognize their parents' song and rush to them to get some food.

There's nothing like a nap after a good meal. This fat chick is too big to fit under its mother.

The chicks change their feathers

In January, the chicks hatch — knock, knock, knock. The sound of the chick trying to break through the shell goes on for two days. After it is out of the shell, the chick stays warm under its parents. A fine gray blanket of feathers begins to grow on its naked body. In three weeks, it has a thick, warm, chocolate-brown coat.

The chicks have no waterproof feathers so they cannot go fishing for food. They have to wait for their parents who go back and forth from their baby to the ocean bringing fish to feed their babies. The parents hold the fish in their throats so the baby has to reach into the parent's mouth to get the fish.

Penguins, fishers of the sea

On the islands where they live, there is nothing to eat, only rocks and a few plants. In the ocean, however, there are millions of fish, and the penguins have a feast.

The shape of a penguin's body and its waterproof feathers are perfect for swimming. They flap their wings to go forward and use their feet to steer. They look like they are flying underwater!

At swimming time, the penguins clean themselves and clown around.

Even though they spend a long time in freezing water, they do not get cold, because they have a thick layer of insulating fat and waterproof feathers.

A huge visitor shares the beach. It is an elephant seal that is 16 feet long and weighs over 3 tons. A penguin weighs only 33 pounds, so to them the elephant seal is gigantic.

To get to the water, penguins must sometimes walk through groups of elephant seals on the beach. These giants come to the land to shed their fur and to have babies. They take up a lot of space!

Two feet and a little tail make a perfect three-footed base to hold the penguin standing up for hours without getting tired.

When looking down at the chicks from above, the difference in their color is clear.

A hard life for a chick

A newborn chick weighs about the same as a large apple. After their parents have fed them for about four months, they weigh about 30 pounds.

In the winter the parents go off to fish, and the babies stay together on land. They squeeze together to protect themselves from the cold. Their parents return to feed them once every few weeks.

The chicks look like teddy bears except for their beaks.

The southern winter

The month of May is not easy in the southern hemisphere. Where we live it is spring and the flowers are in bloom, but where the penguins live, the terrible Antarctic winter begins.

A snow storm starts with fierce winds. The sky is gray and the land is icy. The parents who return to feed their chicks have to fight their way against the strong winds. All the penguins cooperate to keep warm.

A penguin's fat and feathers can keep its body so well insulated that the snowflakes do not melt when they land on its feathers.

To protect themselves from bad weather, they stand with their backs to the wind, forming a triangle shape. The penguins at the center often change places with the penguins at the outer edges of the triangle.

In gusts of wind and snow, the penguins hurry to form a warm group.

In the middle of the resting chicks, a mother calls out to her chick so she can feed it.

It looks like a penguin in disguise, but it is really a chick molting.

Holding on until the end of winter

Finally, it is September, and the weather is warmer. The full grown penguins come back from the ocean.

By October, the chubby chicks begin to lose their chocolate-brown "fur coat" as new feathers appear from underneath. This is called molting.

When the king penguin is two years old, it has an all black beak and yellow, instead of orange, markings.

Return to the colony

A year has passed. At the end of the bad weather, the grown-up penguins have returned to the colony to have babies again. Penguins have only one baby every two years, and they take very good care of it. With an average life span of twenty years, king penguin parents can have several babies.

Penguins are true sea birds. They return to the land only to have and raise their babies or to molt. Most of the time, the penguins are not on land. They are in the water with the fish. What funny birds!

In 1620, when an explorer saw penguins for the first time, he claimed he had discovered "feathered fish"!

Once hunted

Penguins were once hunted, but are now protected by law. Their flocks grow each year. These birds have such an unusual way of life that they are a favorite subject of scientific study. However, because they live in so few areas, people are concerned about their survival.

Scientists tag penguins on their wings, unlike other birds, which are tagged on their feet.

Penguins are not afraid of people. When people are around, the penguins often follow them with curiosity.